Beginning to Subtract

The answer to a subtraction problem is called the difference.

$3 - 1 = 2$

Subtract and write each difference.

$3 - 2 = \square$

$2 - 1 = \square$

$4 - 1 = \square$

$4 - 3 = \square$

$1 - 1 = \square$

$2 - 0 = \square$

Subtraction Using a Number Line for Numbers 1 to 5

$$5 - 3 = 2$$

0 1 2 3 4 5 6 7 8 9 10

Subtract and write each difference.

0 1 2 3 4 5

$3 - 2 =$ 1

0 1 2 3 4 5

$3 - 1 =$ ☐

0 1 2 3 4 5

$4 - 2 =$ ☐

0 1 2 3 4 5

$2 - 2 =$ ☐

0 1 2 3 4 5

$1 - 0 =$ ☐

0 1 2 3 4 5

$5 - 4 =$ ☐

0 1 2 3 4 5 6 7 8 9 10

Subtract and
write each difference.

3 – 3 = ☐ 4 – 4 = ☐

5 – 1 = ☐ 2 – 0 = ☐

5	1	2	3	4
–3	–1	–1	–2	–3
☐	☐	☐	☐	☐

4	5	1	5	4
–0	–2	–0	–5	–1
☐	☐	☐	☐	☐

A-Mazing Subtraction

Subtract to find each difference. Follow the numbers in the order of your answers to help the mother bird feed her babies.

1. $2 - 2 =$
2. $3 - 2 =$
3. $2 - 1 =$
4. $5 - 1 =$
5. $4 - 1 =$
6. $5 - 3 =$
7. $3 - 1 =$
8. $3 - 3 =$
9. $4 - 2 =$
10. $5 - 4 =$
11. $4 - 3 =$
12. $5 - 2 =$

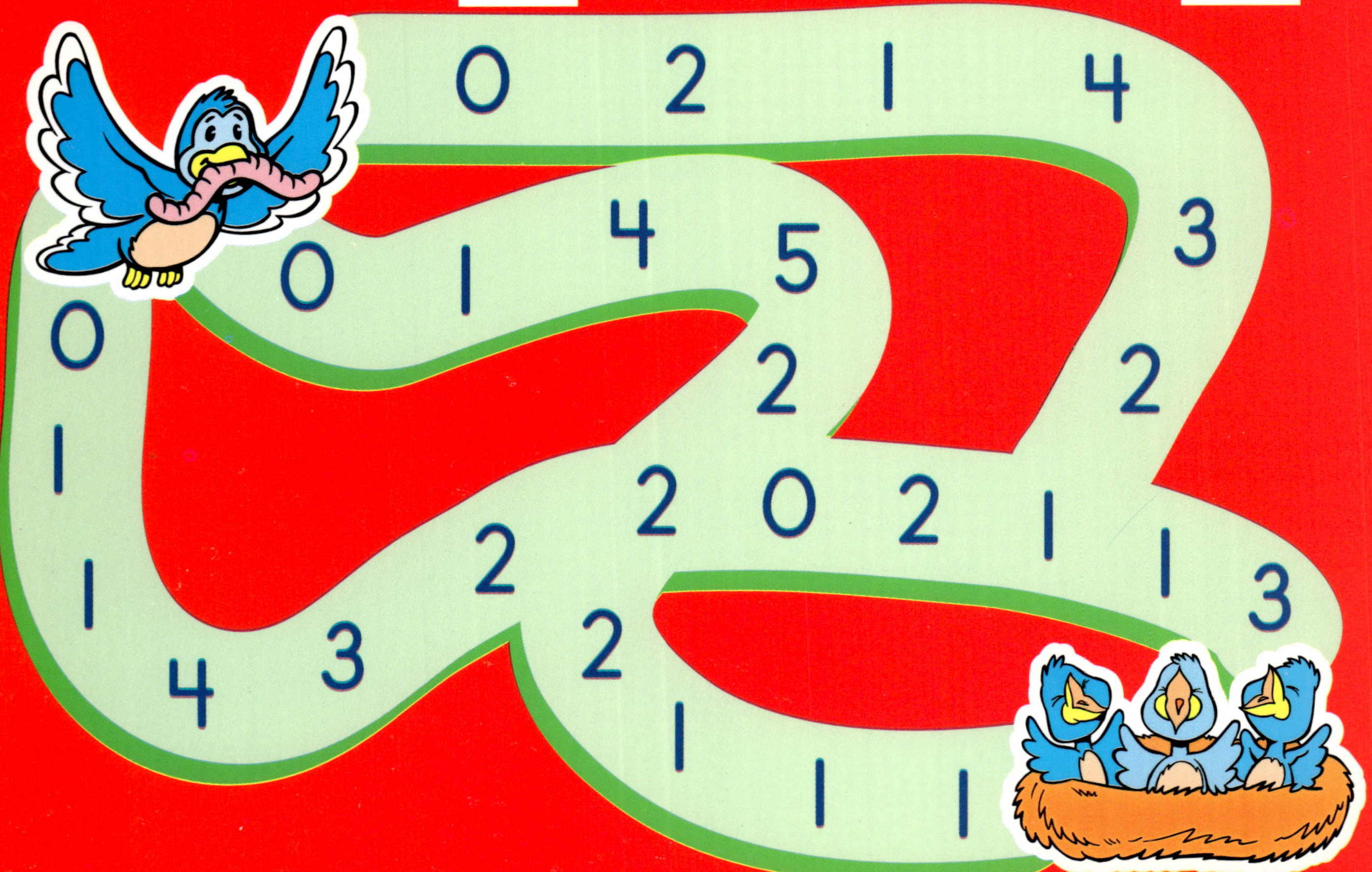

Subtract to Find the Difference

2	5	5	4	5	4
−1	−3	−0	−1	−2	−3

5	4	3	4	3	2
−1	−2	−1	−0	−2	−0

Help the bee take pollen from the flowers to the hive. You can only go to flowers that have the same numbers as your answers. You can connect the answers in any order to reach the hive. Add up the numbers you land on. What is your lowest score?

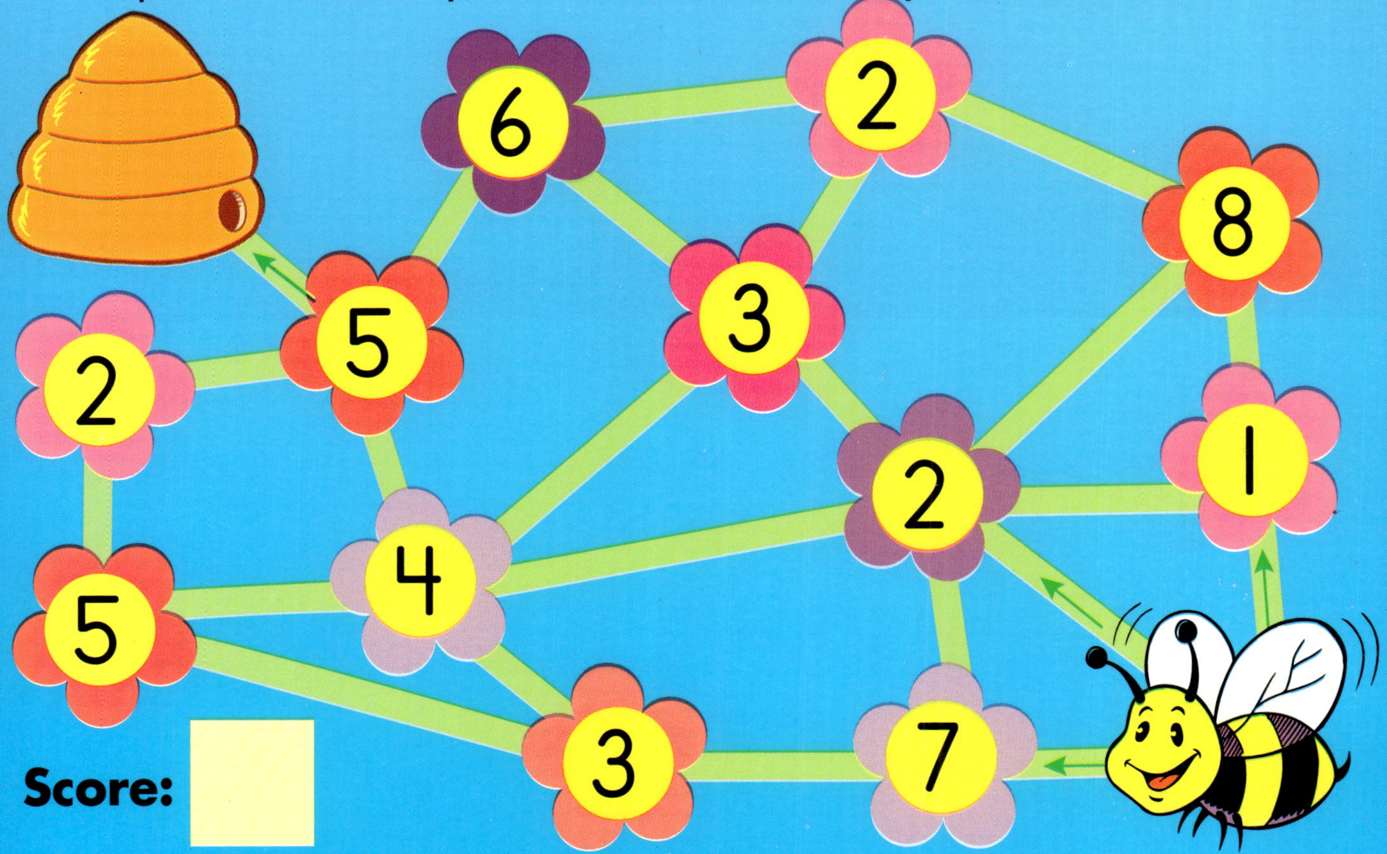

Score:

Subtract with 6 and 7

0 1 2 3 4 5 6 7 8 9 10

Subtract and write each difference.

6	6	6	6	6
−0	−1	−2	−3	−4
☐	☐	☐	☐	☐

6	6	7	7	7
−5	−6	−0	−1	−2
☐	☐	☐	☐	☐

7	7	7	7	7
−3	−4	−5	−6	−7
☐	☐	☐	☐	☐

Subtract

Subtract your way through the maze to take the duck to water.

Subtraction Practice

Subtract. Find and circle the answers in the picture below.

$7 - 6 = \square$	$6 - 4 = \square$	$5 - 2 = \square$	$4 - 4 = \square$	$7 - 3 = \square$
$6 - 1 = \square$	$6 - 0 = \square$	$7 - 0 = \square$		

Subtract each number from the number in the center of the flower. Write the answers on the petals.

Subtract with 8 and 9

Subtract and write each difference.

$8 - 0 = \square$	$8 - 1 = \square$	$8 - 2 = \square$	$8 - 3 = \square$	$8 - 4 = \square$
$8 - 5 = \square$	$8 - 6 = \square$	$8 - 7 = \square$	$8 - 8 = \square$	$9 - 0 = \square$
$9 - 1 = \square$	$9 - 2 = \square$	$9 - 3 = \square$	$9 - 4 = \square$	$9 - 5 = \square$
$9 - 6 = \square$	$9 - 7 = \square$	$9 - 8 = \square$	$9 - 9 = \square$	

Write the missing number to finish each problem.

K	A	E	B	F
$9 - 8 = \square$	$8 - \square = 2$	$9 - \square = 7$	$8 - \square = 5$	$\square - 6 = 2$

Q	X	O	C	U
$9 - \square = 4$	$8 - \square = 4$	$9 - 2 = \square$	$8 - \square = 8$	$\square - 0 = 9$

What do you get when you put 6 ducks in a box?
Match your answers with the letters to find out.

☐   ☐ ☐ ☐   ☐ ☐

6   3 7 4   7 8

☐ ☐ ☐ ☐ ☐ ☐ RS!

5 9 6 0 1 2

Dog-Gone Subtraction

Subtract. Then follow the arrows to help Ned catch his dog.
Add up the numbers you land on.

$8 - 5 = \square$

$\begin{array}{r} 8 \\ -\ 6 \\ \hline \square \end{array}$

$\begin{array}{r} 8 \\ -\ 4 \\ \hline \square \end{array}$

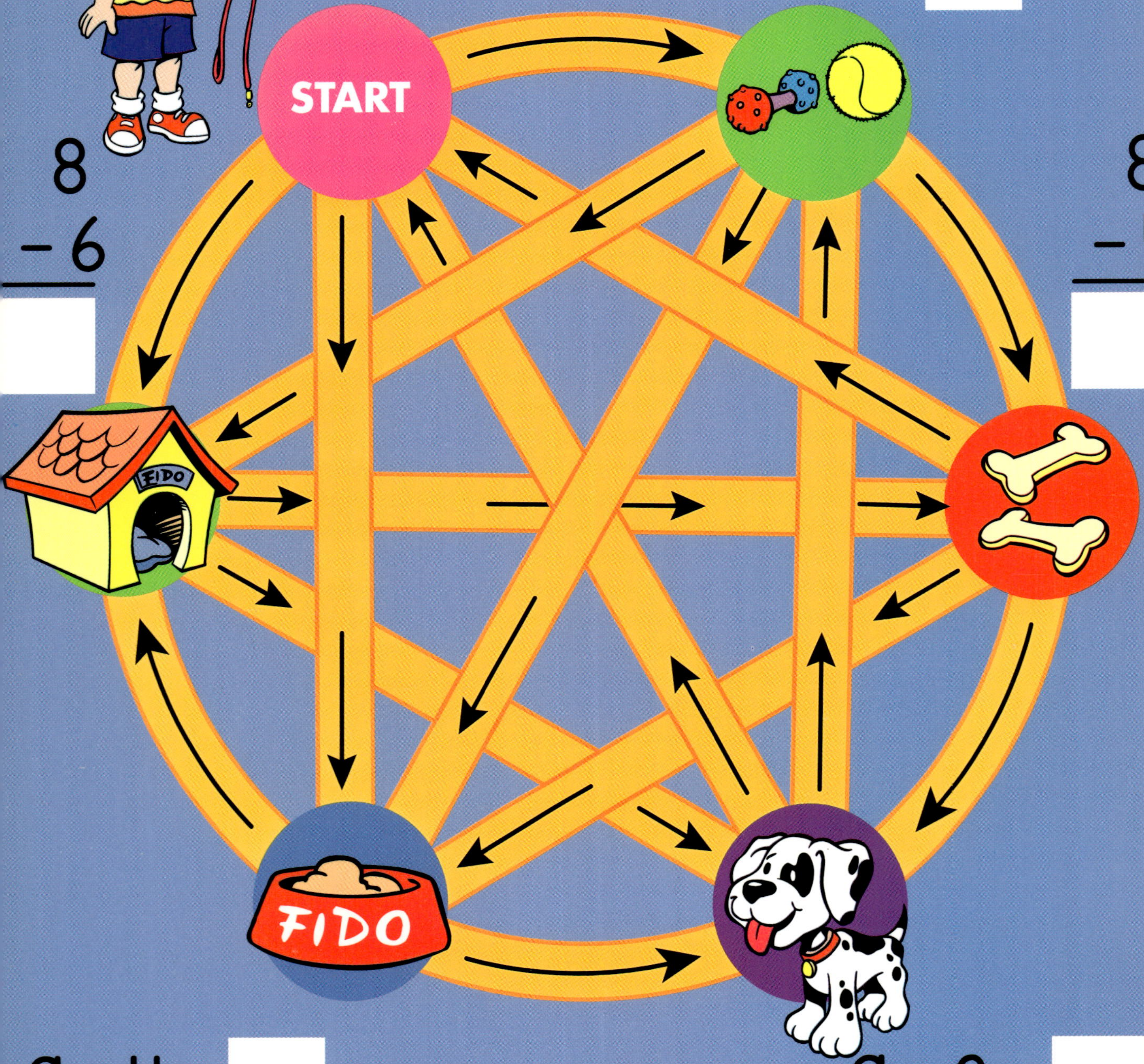

$9 - 4 = \square$

$9 - 3 = \square$

How low can you get your score? $\square$